# Capel Cochineal & Stanley Sheep's School Project "Stroud's String of Pearls"

Tracy Spiers

Mills 1750 - 1820
(cloth)
Meadow
Churchend
Bond's
Stonehouse Mills
Ryeford
Oil
Millend
Beard's
Stanley
Young's
Howell's
"Wow just look at all the pearls!"
Coaley
Holmer
Dauncey's
Draycot
Middle
Cam
upper Cam
Lower
Churn
Townsends
Dauncey's
Jeens
Sheppard's
Howard's
Vizard's
New
Rivers
Dursley
Rockstowes
Marsh
Jackson's
Dauncey's
Newma

Small's
Mills
Upper Steambridge
Lower Steambridge
Rock
Vatch
Wyatt's
Upper Vatch
Rookwood
Badbrook
Hazle
Wades
Peghouse
New
Little
Nashend
Capel's
Arundel
Bowbridge
Newcombe's
Stafford
Griffin's
Roger's
Ham
Toadsmoor
Thrupp
Gough
Woolings
Hope
Gussage
Baker's
Ashmead
Brimscombe
Seville's
Bidmead's
Port
Bourne
Randalls & Spring
Bliss
Chalford
Ills
Ballinger's
St Mary's
Wimberley
Dark
New & Mugmore
Inchbrook
Dunkirk
Egypt
Holcombe
Days
Longford
Georges
Nailsworth
Iron
Avening
"We have such a rich legacy Capel."
And this isn't all of them!

As year 5/6 pupils, we were asked by our class teacher Mrs. Flock-Shoddy to do a project about our local history. The following notes and illustrations are the results of all our research. We hope you appreciate how rich, colourful and inspiring Stroud's wool and water heritage is. Thank you for reading!

Copel and Stanley

First published 2019
The History Press
97 St George's Place, Cheltenham
Gloucestershire, GL50 3QB
www.thehistorypress.co.uk

British Library Cataloguing in Publication Data.
A catalogue record for this book is available from the British Library.

ISBN 978 0 7509 9251 0

Typesetting and origination by Tracy Spiers

"These guys made us famous!"

PEARL = a thing of great rarity and worth.

# Acknowledgements

Capel and Stanley are grateful for all the help, support, time and dedication given by everyone who helped them complete their project. This includes their class teacher Mrs. Flock-Shoddy and head teacher Mr. P. Walker. Special thanks go to Debbie Sleep, Sarah Heague and Lisa Nicholls-Grey at Stroud Valley School for keeping a small red-haired bug supplied with coffee, kindness and for putting up with her quirky humour. Deep

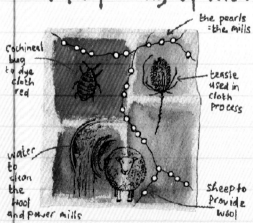

gratitude to Rog, Naomi, Emily, Megan, Rosie and Kezia Spiers, Jan and Bruce Baker and such supportive friends for believing in the book's creator.

Thanks also to Ian Mackintosh and Jane Ford from Stroudwater Textile Trust and The History Press for publishing us.

the pearls = the mills

cochineal bug to dye cloth red

teasle used in cloth process

water to clean the wool and power mills

sheep to provide wool

# Capel Cochineal and Stanley Sheep's

## Introduction to

# The String of Pearls

Stanley

Capel

You will learn lots

# Contents

# Who we are

**Character's Struggle**
Coming to terms with loss of family.

**Character's Role in Mill History**
Provides the dye which made Stroud famous. Ends up being used to clothe kings, soldiers and nobles.

**Origin**
South America on prickly pear plants (cacti).

Capel Cochineal

You have shown great empathy towards your characters

Gullible, struggles with academia, clowning tendencies, generous to others.

**Character Traits**

Gets crushed by life, has too much sun, turns grey and wrinkly, but her death has purpose.

**How Character Changes**

# CHARACTER STUDY

**Character's Struggle**

Feels the cold after woolly coat is shorn off.

**Character's Role in Mill History**

Provides the wool needed to create the broad cloth which helped Stroud become an international success.

**Origin**

Hills of Stroud and Surrounding Cotswold escarpment.

You have made excellent vocabulary choices.

Stanley Sheep

A creature of habit, can be led astray, lets others do hard work, thinks grass is greener else-where.

**Character Traits**

Becomes proud of family achievements, shows empathy to friend and values contribution to Stroud.

**How Character Changes**

2

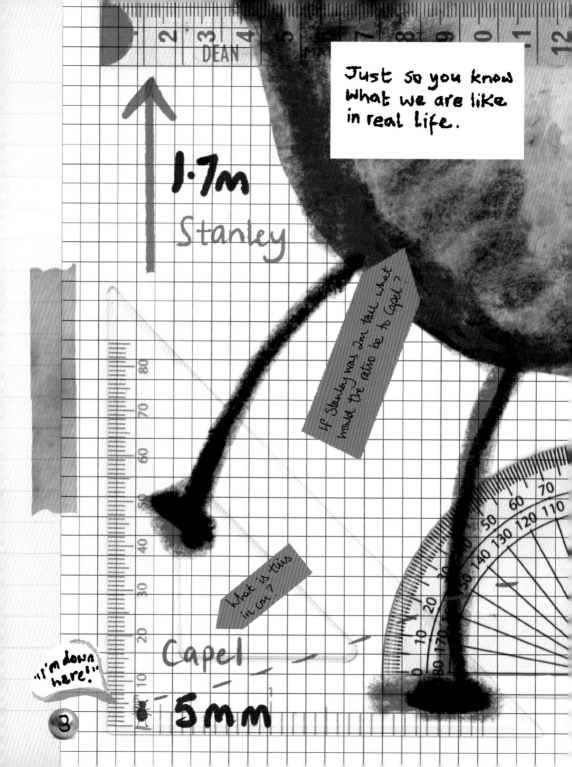

size ratio between us:

Stanley: 1·7m or 1700mm

Capel: 5mm

1700 ÷ 5 = 340

Stanley is 340 x bigger

340 : 1

Great working out.

# Stroud's 'string of pearls'

Stroud once thrived as an important centre for creating woollen cloth. It went all over the world to clothe kings, soldiers and nobles. It evolved here between the Middle Ages and the 1850s. The 'String of Pearls', the collective name for the fine line of mills, is Stroud's most impressive legacy. These 'pearls' were situated next to water and from the air probably looked like jewels on a necklace. They were certainly precious in terms of production, employment, innovation and putting Stroud on the world map for its famous Stroudwater scarlet cloth. The mills once roared with the deafening sound of fulling stocks, waterwheels and spinning jennys. At the height of the woollen industry there were at least 170 working mills in operation along the valley bottom.

"Hey Stanley This former cloth mill was powered by FIVE water wheels."

Great introduction.

a big
← pearl

# Why we had mills

Back in 1086, the Domesday Book which was ordered by King William the Conqueror recorded that Stroud had a number of water-powered mills. It would have certainly been noisy to live next to one.

"That's what you call HEADACHE LOUD!"

"What did you say?"

Good use of dialogue to convey character.

These early mills would have been used to grind corn, making flour for bread. The Normans expected all corn to be ground at the mills belonging to the lord of the Manor rather than in local homes. Mills were later used for corn and fulling.

At the time of the Domesday survey, five corn mills are recorded on Bisley Manor and eight in Minchinhampton. Locally, as elsewhere in the country, it was religious orders who saw opportunities to gain income from fulling mills. They had the resources to adapt corn mills, put up new buildings and create sophisticated watercourses required for the dual function. Gloucestershire's earliest known fulling mill was at Barton in Temple Guiting, dating 1170. In 1270 there were fulling mills in Dudbridge and Wimberley. Closer to Stroud, the monks at Leonard Stanley Priory owned a fulling mill at Millend, Eastington. It was not long before wealthy landowners started installing fulling mills on their land. In the 13th century, Thomas of Rodborough is recorded as owning a fulling mill at Minchinhampton. Wallbridge appears in the 1500s as Walker bridge because of the mill next to it. Although

# We had the right ingredients:

**Fuller's earth**     **Wool**     **Water**

+

liquid gold
(wee)

*find out what fullers earth is used for today*

there are places named Walk and people were called Walkers, the valleys were used because the streams could power the fulling stocks. The act of fulling softens the cloth and fuller's earth was an essential ingredient until soap was increasingly used. It is used today in things like cat litter. Stale urine (known locally as seg), was used to scour or clean out the dirt and grease, mixed historically with pig's dung and pig's blood!

# The five valleys of Stroudwater

Ruscombe

Painswick

Slad

**Stroud**

Chalford

Nailsworth

"See where all the water is— at the valley bottoms!"

Why not walk along one of the five valleys and see what landmarks you can find?

We had water, and water meant POWER. In his book 'Notes and Recollections of Stroud,' (1871) P.H. Fisher names the five valleys as:

Stroud had lots of sheep!

Cuckold's brook (Ruscombe brook joins the Frome at Dudbridge), Painswick (Painswick Stream joins the Frome at Lodgemore), Slad and Steanbridge, Stroud and Chalford, and finally Rodborough, Woodchester and Nailsworth. Our map simplifies this.

The limestone hilltops provided a perfect pasture for sheep and an ideal building material, whilst layers of clay created the springs – perfect for fresh water for nearby cottages and to turn the waterwheels. As for the clay, known as Fuller's earth, this was ideal for cleaning the cloth.

In the Middle Ages, the cloth was made by weavers and to make it weatherproof, it was thickened or shrunk by men walking on it for hours in vats of urine (wee).

The surnames Tucker, Walker and Fuller refer to this form of hard and smelly labour!

15

This was a horrible job which continued until fulling stocks were introduced. These were enormous loud hammers which pounded the cloth in a mix of water, urine and Fuller's earth.

Can you write a list of synonyms of synonyms for 'horrible'?

"Ow! my ears!"

Stroud has had fulling stocks since at least the late 1200s

# Dye Plants

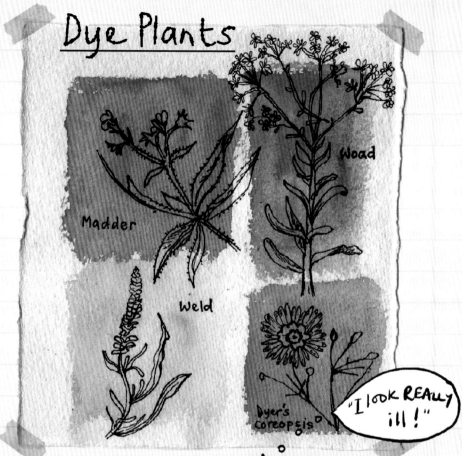

Madder

Woad

Weld

Dyer's coreopsis

"I look REALLY ill!"

Can you have a go at dyeing your own wool or fabric? What colours will you use?

Cloth got dyed using natural plants found in the local area. The leaf and stem of weld created a yellow dye. Woad, part of the

cabbage family,
produced blue dye
which was extracted
from the leaves. 
Uley Blue was
the name of
a local
cloth,
so called because of
its distinctive shade. 
Dyer's Coreopsis
had flowers of
yellow and deep red
and produced
an orange.

"I'm either
very cold or
feeling blue."

"I'm environmentally
friendly — I've gone
green!"

"There's no
place like home!"

Madder was the
plant much sought
after because of
the strength of
its red, which was
unusual among plant dyes.

18

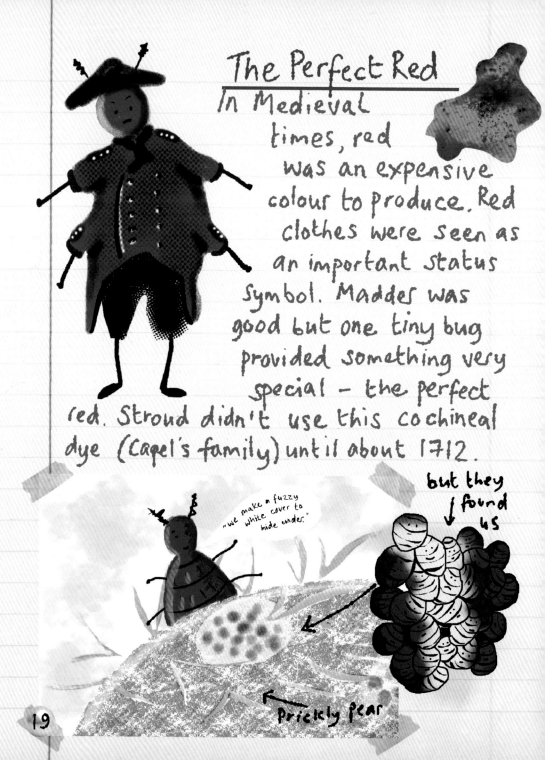

# The Perfect Red

In Medieval times, red was an expensive colour to produce. Red clothes were seen as an important status symbol. Madder was good but one tiny bug provided something very special — the perfect red. Stroud didn't use this cochineal dye (Capel's family) until about 1712.

"we make a fuzzy white cover to hide under."

but they found us

prickly pear

pretend
bug juice

bug we
made for
illustration

*Can you research and produce a fact file on a famous explorer?*

(N.B. No cochineal bugs were harmed as part of our project.)
In the 16th century, the discovery of the Americas by Spanish explorers opened up a rich new world, previously unknown in Europe. One of those riches was cochineal, found on prickly pear cactus plants growing in Mexico. Unlike madder, which faded, cochineal produced a deeper and long-lasting red due to its chemical composition. It was a 'wow' word and a 'wow' colour!

# Destined to DYE

Fact: important Capel's family! →

It takes about 154,000 dead cochineal bugs to make one kilogram (1kg) of dye.

That's the same as 7 medium apples; a bag of sugar or rice; a loaf and a half of bread; a thousand paperclips; a small watermelon or a pineapple. Be warned because cochineal, also known as Carmine or E120 can be found in drinks, cosmetics and foods. Best check!

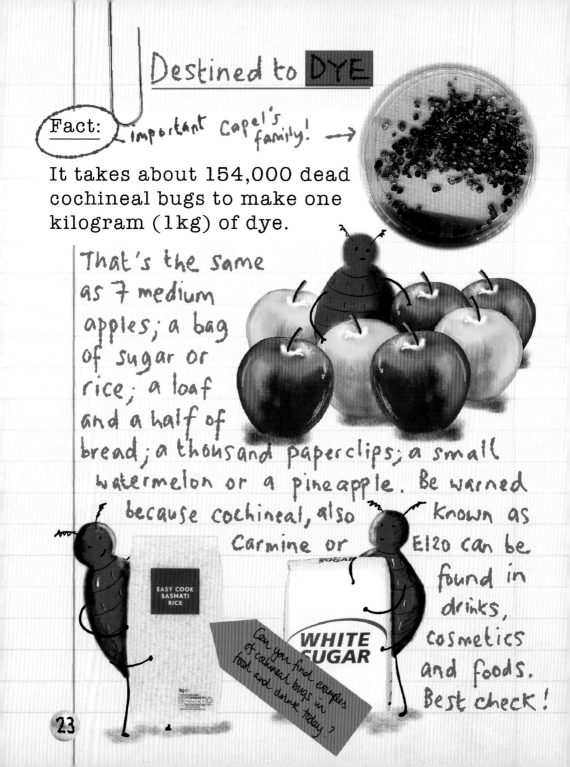

EASY COOK BASMATI RICE

WHITE SUGAR

Can you find examples of cochineal bugs in food and drink today?

23

Scarlet colouring was a secret and arrived in Stroud in the early 18th century. A Dutchman discovered that putting tin in the cochineal made the scarlet. He kept the recipe TOP SECRET and only in 1610 opened his business at Bow Mill, East London. It developed here until the secret got out. First references for scarlet cloth being made in Stroud is around 1712 when local clothiers presented the future George I with a roll of scarlet and the future George II with a roll of crimson, also made with cochineal. It was worth 45 shillings a yard, compared to madder, which was about four. "Never has finer cloth been made in England," reported Daniel Defoe.

King George I
1714-1727

"What a gorgeous colour."

King George II
1727-1760

"Most kind."

# Destined to DYE continued

The demand for red dye was due to the growing number of wars taking place. One example was the Napoleonic Wars (1803-15). Dye was used for military uniforms. Thousands of soldiers would have worn the famous Stroudwater Scarlet. Ironically and sadly many died like the bugs.

Incidentally, another George, King George III had a Stroud connection. He visited in 1788 while he was recovering from ill health at the Spa town of Cheltenham. He rode on horseback to see a mill at Woodchester. He also visited the junction of Stroud's two new canals.

"I am NOT short!"

Napoleon had an issue →

How tall was Napoleon?

"Stroud - how lovely."

King George III
1760 - 1820

Cochineal was used in Stroud for hundreds of years despite the introduction of synthetic dye. In 1856, an 18 year old chemistry student called William Perkin accidentally discovered the first synthetic dye, known as mauveine. It was referred to as 'Perkin's Mauve.' The Victorians loved it. Queen Victoria even wore purple at her eldest daughter Victoria's wedding. Cochineal was harder to make synthetically unlike Indigo which was easier. It continued first at Bowbridge then at Cam until the 1960s because the Ministry of Defence insisted upon it. These two cochineal dyeing mills were probably the last in the world!

26

NORTH
AMERICA

NORTH
ATLANTIC
OCEAN

EUROP

AFRICA

SOUTH
AMERICA

SOUTH
ATLANTIC
OCEAN

PACIFIC
OCEAN

SOUTHERN

"My ancestors travelled 55,000 miles
to provide dye. Stroud got its dye from Bow
Mills in East London, so I could be a Cockney!"

It wasn't just the cochineal bugs who travelled here. Many woollen mills are linked with families of Flemish weavers who fled to England following religious persecution in the 15th and 16th centuries. Names associated with these original Huguenot families include the Haigs, Prouts, Clutterbucks, Playnes and Pauls.

ASIA

PACIFIC OCEAN

INDIAN OCEAN

AUSTRALASIA

also known as Oceania

N

ANTARCTICA

No planes then

Stroudwater cloth

ancestors' journey

PLEASE LOOK AFTER THIS BUG

"Not one Prickly Pear take-away in sight"

Can you write a journal from the perspective of an immigrant embarking on this journey, how did they feel leaving their home?

28

# Cloth making started at home

1. <u>Wash</u> <u>the</u> <u>wool</u> (without the sheep)

"SOAP please Capel!"

Can you research a process and write an explanation text?

"Will I sleep for 100 years?"

5. <u>Spinning</u> - this stretches fibres out and twists them to form yarn.

↰ done by women, hence where name 'spinster' from comes

## 2. Sort and grade the wool.

"I feel naked!"

Wool is sorted and graded

Stanley's coat

## 3. Combing - similar to carding; leaves fibres straighter.

done by child

## 4. Carding - this means untangling the new fleece with two boards covered in metal spikes.

## The weaver's role

Once the yarn was ready, it was handed to the weaver. Stroud's broadcloth, woven 10 feet wide required two men or a wife and son to weave. Spinning was done in agricultural areas – wool from Fromehall Mill was sent to Frampton on Severn or agricultural parts of Painswick where women organised carding and spinning.

In the 1720s the Capels at Capel Mill had a spinning house at Prestbury.

31

Cloth making was a family business — a cottage industry — and weavers enjoyed their independence.

Once woven, the cloth had to be taken to the nearby mill often down steep slopes to the valley bottom on pack horses. Here it was finished and underwent scouring, fulling, drying, gigging,

"Are we nearly there yet Stanley?"

"Stop moaning Capel!"

shearing, dyeing and pressing. Weavers working in their cottages were known as out-weavers. Their role was threatened by the Industrial Revolution.

# Finishing process of cloth

Woven cloth was folded and put in the mill's fulling stocks, with water, fuller's earth and stale urine.
These large hammers thumped the cloth until it was shrunk by a third of its original size. In the 1800s this could have taken up to 24 hours. It is like putting a woollen jumper in a modern-day washing machine at too high a temperature. The cloth shrinks as heat creates friction. Fibres are also loosened and makes it easier to raise the nap. As the cloth is now wet, it has to be stretched out to dry.

shrunk in wash

Write a story about a sock that shrinks in the wash.

33

# 'On tenterhooks'

Cloth could be seen drying out in fields around Stroud, notably blue, white and the famous red. It was put on tenter frames and kept taut by tenterhooks to prevent it from shrinking as it dried. Tenter comes from the Latin word 'tendere', meaning to stretch. The phrase 'on tenterhooks' was introduced in the 1750s to mean being in a state of tension or anxiety.

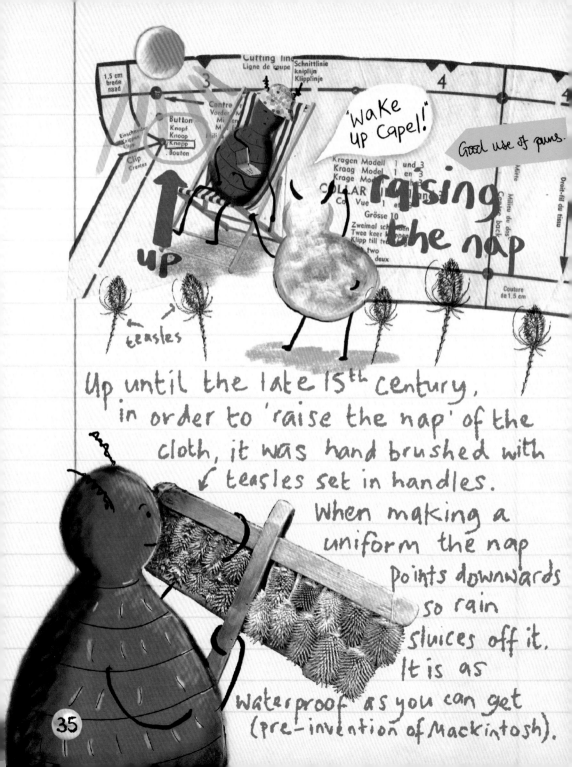

'Wake up Capel!'

Good use of puns.

**raising the nap**

up

teasles

Up until the late 15th century, in order to 'raise the nap' of the cloth, it was hand brushed with teasles set in handles.

When making a uniform the nap points downwards so rain sluices off it. It is as waterproof as you can get (pre-invention of Mackintosh).

Napping (NOT sleeping) is part of the finishing process in cloth making, which raises fibres to produce a nap, or mat of fibre ends.

The Gig was the second water-powered machine used in the mills. Stroud began using it in the 1550s. Later improvements continued throughout the subsequent centuries. Teasles were used locally until the 1970s.

teasles packed tightly

Can you find a teasle and draw it.

"The fluff is getting up my nose!"

# The shearmen

It was the job of the shearmen to trim the nap to ensure the broadcloth had a smooth and even finish. They were one of the highest paid workers in the mill, earning 24 shillings a week - that was until the Industrial Revolution. ✓ real stuff

*Shearing or Cutting.*—This operation is to shear or cut the pile raised by the gig-mill to an even and a close surface. Formerly this operation was performed by shearmen, who passed the shears over the cloth, which was tightly stretched upon an inclined plane. The shears weighed from 30lbs. to 40lbs., and consisted of two blades, one, the larger blade, resting on the cloth, the other, a moveable blade, and nearly perpendicular, worked by the shearer's hand, and at each blow it removed a certain portion of the pile.

This labour was performed by two men whose wages were about 24s. a-week each man. It was a laborious operation, and only applicable to the coarse manner in which cloth was then manufactured for the market. This plan was superseded about forty years ago by an improved plan, namely, placing the shears in a frame, which travelled over the cloth, and cut or sheared it as by hand.

"I need to keep ALL of my hands steady for this job!"

write an emotional piece of writing about the impact of this machine on a shearman.

Written by W. A. Miles c1839 Hand-loom Weavers Report

up to 40 lbs the report says, that's about 18kg or
- 120 bananas
- 180 blueberry muffins
- 30 pairs of court shoes
32 basket balls
or 600 roses!

However according to Mr. Miles, they were not always very well behaved.

The shearmen, before the introduction of machines in that department, were notorious for their drunken and careless habits. They would sometimes refuse to work when they knew that their employer was under contract and penalties as to time, unless he gave them drink; and it was to clear themselves from these drunken dictatorial liabilities that the manufacturers eagerly adopted the use of machinery to rid themselves of the shearmen.

The cross cutter developed between 1815-18 by John Lewis of Brimscombe Mills. It was a direct threat to the shearmen's livelihoods. It quickly replaced them as this new machine could do their job much more evenly and faster. By 1829 Lewis claimed that he had already sold thousands of his rotary shearing device and soon they were used all over the world.

It took a good mathematical brain to work this out!

Two of Lewis' Machines were operated by a man and a boy.

long cylinder with a revolving spiral blade

38

Edwin
Beard
Budding

## STROUD INVENTIONS

**1796** Edward Jenner from Berkeley tests vaccine for smallpox on 8-year-old James Phipps, who recovers from the disease.
**1837** Isaac Pitman from Wotton-under-Edge invents shorthand.
**1893** Mikael Pedersen, a Danish inventor living in Dursley designs the Pedersen bicycle.

Born in Eastington, Stroud in 1796, Edwin Beard Budding was an innovative engineer who invented the world's first lawnmower in his home town in 1830. The idea came from the Perpetual which drew the cloth lengthwise through the stationary cutter instead of cutting across the cloth.

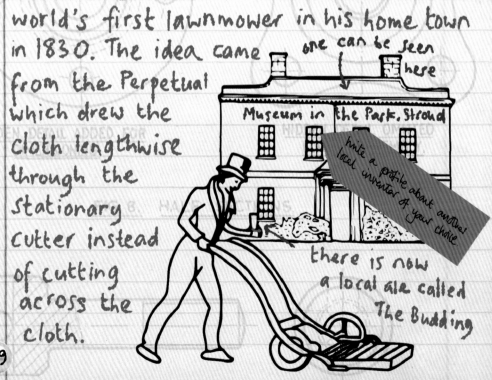

one can be seen here

Museum in the Park, Stroud

write a profile about another local inventor of your choice

there is now a local ale called The Budding

Together with local engineer John Ferrabee, Budding made mowers at the Phoenix Iron Works at Thrupp. To avoid curiosity, Budding tested his first cutting machine at night. Ferrabee financed the patenting and manufacturing costs. Budding

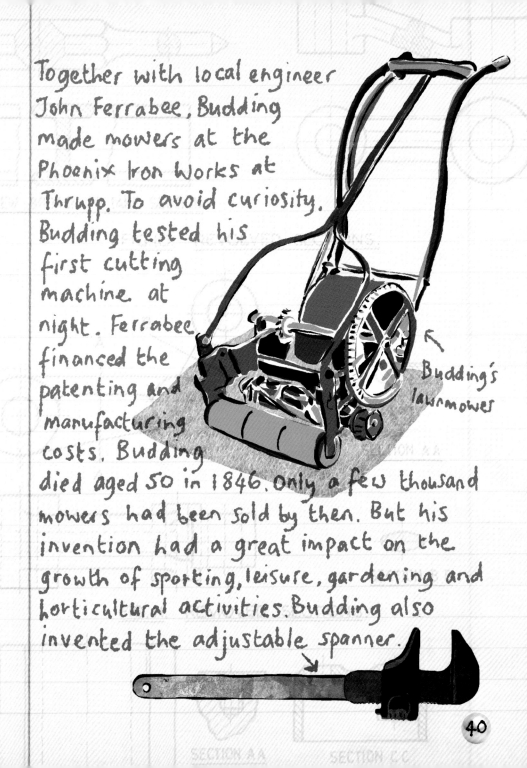

Budding's lawnmower

died aged 50 in 1846. Only a few thousand mowers had been sold by then. But his invention had a great impact on the growth of sporting, leisure, gardening and horticultural activities. Budding also invented the adjustable spanner.

# The Industrial Revolution

" " " " "
"I'm a bit dizzy!"
"
"

James Hargreaves' Spinning Jenny 1764

Richard Arkwright's Water Frame Spinning Machine 1769

This was the age of change, innovation and expansion which impacted almost every aspect of life. The arrival of new machinery and technology made a profound change both economically, socially, professionally and culturally. The world literally was in a spin as Capel demonstrates. New innovations in machinery expanded the mills meaning an end to the cottage industry for many. Whole families - spinners, weavers and their children - became mill workers.

The Industrial Revolution also saw the arrival of STEAM. Up until the 18<sup>th</sup> century, the country's main power source had been

James Watt's steam engines 1775/6

wood. However coal could produce up to three times more energy. The population was growing and the demand for coal was great. Engineers and inventors looked at new ways to source this fuel. It led to the steam engine which could pump water from hundreds of metres underground. It was a time of great ideas and discoveries.

Great work.

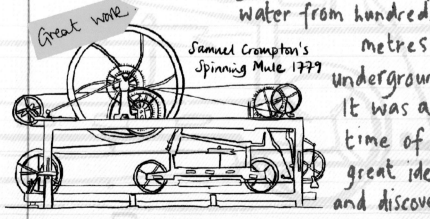

Samuel Crompton's Spinning Mule 1779

# Building the canals

The Industrial Revolution resulted in huge amounts of heavy produce such as coal and iron, which had to be moved large distances. Canals became the answer. Throughout the 1700s until the late 1800s, canal routes thrived and played a huge part in supplying the Stroud valleys with fuel and raw materials. The Stroudwater Canal was built in 1779 and the Thames & Severn Canal in 1789. They helped the world connect to Stroud's industries and vice versa. Locks,

Write a descriptive piece about a day in the life of a navvy

"It's a tough life being a navvy!"

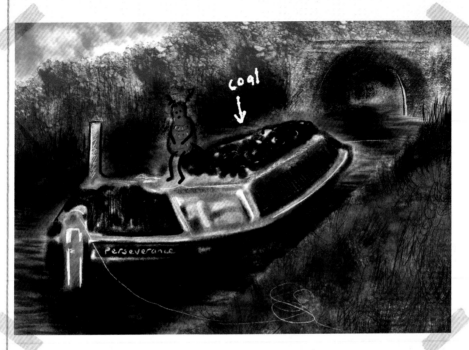

bridges, tunnels and aqueducts were designed
by engineers to overcome problems of uneven
terrain and were dug out by navigators,
known as navvies. Locks, which used gravity
to move water through the lock gates, enabled
boats to travel up and down hills. (There's a
lot in Stroud!) However by the 1880s, both
canals suffered from railway and competition.
Eventually they became derelict. Today, they
are being restored for a new purpose. - leisure.

## Then came the railway...

Stroud's cloth makers were enthusiastic supporters of train travel. They knew they could get their cloth to London much easier by rail so they invited prestigious engineer Isambard Kingdom Brunel down to Stroud to persuade him. A public meeting was held in the Subscription Rooms in 1834 where he was invited to speak – before a single shovelful of earth had been moved on the Great Western line. Stroud finally got its railway in 1845. The first ever steam-powered train arrived in 1825. It was the Stockton to Darlington line built by George Stephenson in Yorkshire.

the age of steam

# Queen Victoria steams by!

"So this is Stroud! I must come and visit one day!"

...but she never did.

Queen Victoria was a great railway fan. Apparently she spent $10,000 a year on train travel! She passed by Stroud in 1849 on her journey back from London to Balmoral. She had to change at Gloucester. Write a letter persuading Brunel to come to Stroud. Isambard Kingdom Brunel was one of the most prolific engineers in history. Stroud's railway station and goods shed were his works. The latter is now used for a variety of artistic and educational projects.

# Jobs in the mills

Due to the different stages involved in making woollen cloth, there was a plethora of jobs available - some more skilled and better paid than others. Mill workers had to 'clock in' and were expected to work up to 13 hours a day.

They then faced a long walk home, often up hill. Life in the mills was tough. It was cold, smelly, dark, excruciatingly noisy and quite dangerous. Some clothiers were kinder than others.

Apply for a job in the mill.

mule scavenger

STATEMENT of the AVERAGE EARNINGS of different CLASSES of WORKPEOPLE connected with the Manufacture of WOOLLEN CLOTH, in the County of GLOUCESTER, from the Year 1808 to 1838, showing the Decrease per Cent. in the Wages of each Class.

| DESCRIPTION OF WORKPEOPLE. | By whom the labour is performed. | AMOUNT OF EARNINGS. | | | | | | | Total Decrease per Cent. |
|---|---|---|---|---|---|---|---|---|---|
| | | 1808 to 1815. | 1816 to 1818. | 1819 to 1823. | 1829 to 1835. | 1836. | 1837. | 1838. | |
| | | s. d. | s. d. | s. d. | s. d. | s. d. | s. d. | s. d. | |
| 1. Sorters | Men | 30 0 | 30 0 | 30 0 | 30 0 | 30 0 | 30 0 | 30 0 | |
| 2. Scourers | Men | 15 0 | 15 0 | 14 0 | 13 0 | 13 0 | 13 0 | 13 0 | 13 |
| 3. Beaters and Pickers | Women | 8 0 | 7 0 | 6 0 | 6 0 | 5 6 | 5 6 | 5 6 | 31 |
| 4. Engine Man | Men | .. | .. | 24 0 | 24 0 | 24 0 | 24 0 | 24 0 | |
| 5. Feeders to Scribblers | Children | 4 0 | 4 0 | 3 6 | 3 0 | 3 0 | 3 0 | 3 0 | 25 |
| 6. " " Carders | Children | 4 0 | 4 0 | 3 6 | 3 6 | 3 6 | 3 6 | 3 6 | 12 |
| 7. Roller Joiners | Children | 3 0 | 3 0 | 3 0 | 3 0 | 2 6 | 2 6 | 2 0 | 34 |
| 8. Slubber or Abb Spinner | Man | 24 0 | 23 0 | 22 0 | 21 0 | 20 0 | 20 0 | 20 0 | 17 |
| 9. Spinner at the jenny | Women | 14 0 | 14 0 | 12 0 | 10 0 | 8 0 | 7 0 | 6 0 | 57 |
| 10. Mule Spinners* | Men | .. | .. | 25 0 | 25 0 | 22 0 | 22 0 | 22 0 | 12 |
| 11. Mule Piecers | Women | .. | .. | 6 0 | 5 0 | 5 0 | 5 0 | 5 0 | 18 |
| 12. Warpers | Women | 10 0 | 9 0 | 8 0 | 7 0 | 7 0 | 7 0 | 7 0 | 30 |
| 13. Master Weavers† | Men Women | 16 0 | 16 0 | 13 0 | 12 0 | 11 0 | 10 0 | 10 0 | 37·5 |
| 14. Millmen | Men | 21 0 | 21 0 | 20 0 | 20 0 | 20 0 | 20 0 | 20 0 | |
| 15. Burlers | Women | 10 0 | 10 0 | 10 0 | 7 0 | 6 0 | 6 0 | 6 0 | 40 |
| 16. Rowers or Roughers | Men | 21 0 | 24 0 | 24 0 | | | 24 0 | 24 0 | |
| 17. Dyers | Men | 24 0 | 24 0 | 20 0 | | | | 12 0 | 50 |
| 18. Cutters | Men | 21 0 | 20 0 | 20 0 | | | | 13 0 | 38 |
| 19. Brushers | Men | 15 0 | 15 0 | 15 0 | | | | | 7 |
| 20. Markers and Drawers | Women | 10 0 | 10 0 | 9 0 | | | | | 20 |
| 21. Pressers and Packers | Men | 18 0 | 18 0 | 16 0 | | | | | |

\* The mules have superceded the jennies.

The factory weaver averages about 11s 9d per week and the outdoor master weaver 8s 1d. ... including all play or waiting time.

# THE PAPER MILL

## Reporting news about the String of Pearls in the Stroud Valleys and beyond

*Pretend to be a reporter and interview one of the angry outweavers. What questions would you ask?*

# WEAVERS STRIKE OVER POOR PAY

### 1833

Angry outweavers working in the Nailsworth valley went on strike, demanding higher wages. Owner of Dunkirk Mill, Peter Playne won a large contract to produce a significant amount of cloth but refused to pay employees wages they were expecting.

### tension

The years leading up to this event, were full of tension at the mill. Playne had pushed many of his hand-loom weavers to give up their independence of working at home. A huge loomshop was built in 1828 which Playne claimed housed 60 looms and more were installed at Iron Mills, near Longfords,

a mill owned by his brother William. Although 156 had become shop-weavers, Playne still had more than 280 outweavers in their cottages scattered across 10 parishes to call upon when bigger orders came in.

### bitter

During the 1833 strike, bitter arguments continued for seven weeks until the men finally gave up and had to accept the wages on offer. The contract did get finished but at a financial loss which left Mr. Playne frustrated and angry. Industrial unrest such as this led to the formation of trade unions.

*Better treatment*

49

# THE PAPER MILL

## IN POLITICS

### FACTORY ACTS

Social reformer Lord Shaftesbury persuaded Parliament to pass the Factory Act in 1833. This meant only children aged nine and above could now work in mills. They were restricted to work no more than nine hours a day while 13-18 years were not allowed to work more than 12 hours. It also made it compulsory for children to receive two hours of education a day.

The Factory Act of 1844 improved life for children further, stopping children aged nine to 13 from working more than six and a half hours a day.

### EDUCATION ACTS

This act in 1880 made school compulsory for all children aged between five and 10. The Education Act in 1902 established a system of secondary schools.

## EMIGRATION

The birth of the factory mills marked the end of the hand weavers era. To many of the cottage workers, life in the mill seemed like a prison sentence. But with the arrival of steam and power looms, the change was inevitable. It resulted in smaller mills closing down and there was simply not enough jobs for everyone. During 1828 and 1840, a huge number of outweavers chose to emigrate rather than stay and risk being sent to the workhouse. Whole communities disappeared. In Uley, up to 1,000 people left. Weavers in the Bisley, Horsley, Cam and Hampton parishes also emigrated. And in the Nailsworth area, some 300 cottages were left empty as families sought work in Yorkshire Mills, Kidderminster carpet-making, Witney blankets; and abroad such as Australia, New Zealand and America.

write an editorial comment from the outweavers point of view

# Stroud cloth wrapped around the world

casino cloth

army uniform

Victorian frock coats

naval uniform

billiard cloth

tennis balls

Visit Stroud's Museum in the Park to find more examples of Stroud cloth.

Stroud's broadcloth was eventually traded all over the world. It was used by the British army, but it also became an important commodity in the Americas, Burma, Japan, India and Europe.

Local cloth was sent to North America by the Hudson's Bay Company and across Asia by the East India Company. By the late 1600s, Bristol ships took it to America to be exchanged for furs, and in Canada for beaver skins. It was said a successful hunter would name his squaw (now an offensive term) 'Stroud' to demonstrate his skill. The fabric known as 'Strouds' was used instead of animal hide. It was dyed and an ideal backdrop for decorating with beads, quiltwork or appliqué silk ribbons. It was used as flashes for weapons, trousers, blankets and moccasins.

## Stroud Wrapped Around The World continued

In Burma, the Akha people used very fine Stroud Scarlet wool cloth as part of their appliqué decoration on ornate leggings worn by women. Stroud cloth also went to Portugal and Spain, Germany and Russia. It was sent into the country, for example, in Shropshire, a lady had a red Stroudwater petticoat fringed with lace. This was made with madder.

Part of Burmese traditional dress

Stroud Scarlet

Super effort.

Blue was originally made with woad grown locally. But the best was imported from France. Samuel Yeates, a woodster, lived at Dyehouse Mill in the Nailsworth valley. He died around 1680 and left a small fortune. Indigo was being used at the same time in the Uley area – hence the name Uley Blue. A stronger blue and more expensive, it was used with woad or for very expensive blue such as officers in the

Royal Navy by the 1800s. When black became fashionable in Victorian times, Samuel Marling made lots of money selling high quality black as well as blue cloth dyed at Stanley Mill. Logwood from South America was used to make the dye, not a black sheep!

Victorian frock coat made with Stroud cloth

And a bit about the East India Company. This was founded in 1599 and became the largest company in the world. It first sent cloth to the Spice Islands, bits of Indonesia, then to India, then to China. Leonard Holliday of Rodborough, later Mayor of London and Sir Leonard, was a founding member. In October 1815, 78 manufacturers from the Stroud valleys supplied nearly £40,000 worth of cloth - that's nearly £2 million today.

# What happened to the pearls?

During the Industrial Revolution, when new canals, railways and steamships helped with the carrying of raw materials and finished products, the mill industry in Stroud was at its peak. Wars overseas meant cloth for Stroudwater Scarlet was in demand.

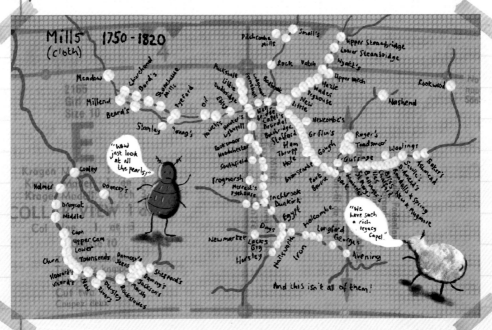

This map gives a flavour of the landscape, but it doesn't show all the mills. However it does help visualise the 'string of pearls.'

Yet fast forward to modern day and it all looks (and sounds) very different. Out of those original 170 pearls, only two are still operating in wool production, namely Cam and Lodgemore Mills. So what happened? Why did Stroud lose the other pearls? Competition from Yorkshire Mills meant we lost major

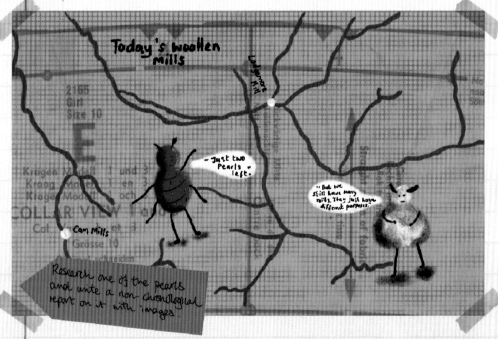

Today's woollen mills

Lodgemore Hill

~ Just two Pearls ~ left.

"But we still have many mills. They just have different purposes."

Cam Mills

Research one of the pearls and write a non-chronological report on it with images.

orders; the end of the French wars left many clothiers bankrupt and mills were either shut down or used for other industries.

## Later mill industries

Although Stroud mourned the loss of its broad cloth, its prosperity was restored as woollen mills were adapted accommodating new industries. Smaller mills such as those in the Painswick and Slad valleys were used for bone grinding, flour or saw milling; while larger mills became flock and shoddy mills such as Capel's, Toadsmoor and Merrett's. Flock is torn up cloth or wool waste used as soft material for stuffing cushions or quilts. Shoddy is inferior yarn (i.e. not up

FLOCK and SHODDY

to standard), made by shredding scraps of woollen rags into fibres, which are then ground and mixed with small amounts of new wool. It's a good example of early recycling and started in Batley, Yorkshire around 1813 with the rag and bone man collecting rags in the streets. Making shoddy created a very fine dust, used for manure on fields. Some shoddy workers suffered from shoddy fever as they breathed in the dust.

About 20 mills in the Stroud area became centres for stick manufacture which included walking sticks and parasols.

## Later mill industries continued

Frogmarsh, Inchbrook and several mills in Painswick started manufacturing pins. At Wimberley Mills, Brimscombe, hairpins and knitting needles were also made. Some woollen mills continued in the textile vein, by throwing silk for a while. Phoenix Ironworks was housed at Thrupp Mill, Dudbridge Ironworks was set up in 1891 to make oil and gas engines and Lightpill Mill became a major producer for plastics, called Casein, made from cows' milk curd. Brimscombe Mills became a creator of gyroscopic compasses for the Royal Navy while New Mills in Wotton-under-Edge started manufacturing inspection and

"I just can't decide what to have!"

measurement equipment. Ebley Mill is now home to Stroud District Council and Ebley Oil Mill, which got converted to a flour mill post woollen days, is now Snow Business, an international success story. It makes artificial snow for the film and television industry. Other modern uses include restaurants like Egypt Mill; private homes and flats, art studios, galleries, and fitness. Capel regularly runs at the Fitness Mill (Griffin Mill).

Snow Business

# Today's pearls - the last two

"Hey, this is an ace game!"

Fantastic illustrations.

 Today, Lodgemore and Cam Mills, now known as WSP Textiles still produce fine cloth for the sports and leisure industry. WSP specialises in manufacturing in coverings for tennis balls, snooker and pool tables. The company partners with big names such as Dunlop and Slazenger. WSP stands for Winterbotham, Strachan

61

and Playne. The Strachan family bought
Lodgemore Mills in 1865, now the company's
operational site and headquarters. The
Strachan of Stroud trademark was first
registered in 1890 and this brand is now
the benchmark in quality for snooker and
pool. Playne's is its tennis brand, dating
back to 1759 when the Playne family bought
mills in the Stroud valleys. Modern day
woven tennis felt was originally made at
Longfords. WSP's cloth is used at the World
Snooker Championships and Wimbledon. It
sells cloth to over 40 countries.

# When the rivers ran red and blue

river water

When Stroud's mills were in full working order, the rivers used to run red and blue etc. The mill pond below Lodgemore in 1910 was often jet black with dye but the swans swam in it still pure white! Development of synthetic dyes

killed off the river life so the law changed and Longfords spent £50,000 making a water cleansing system. That was the beginning of the recovery and today our rivers and canals are thriving habitats for wildlife. Kingfishers, damselflies, herons, otters, dragonflies, bats and an early morning deer have been spotted along these waterways.

Take a walk down the canal and draw a lock.

# Extra facts

Prince Philip's Naval wedding uniform was made and dyed at Lodgemore Mill in 1947.

The Russian Royal family wore cloth made at Stonehouse Upper Mills.

Cloth for the Pope was last supplied on his visit in 1984.

In 1820 Longfords Mill was Britain's largest broadcloth supplier to the East India Company. Laid end to end, the 5,000 cloths, each 36 yards long, would have stretched 102 miles, from the mill to their London office. It was worth £56,000.

Ronald Reagan, the former President of the USA, was shot wearing a suit of Stroud-made cloth.

A kazoo band formed by workers at Longford's Mill won a competition in 1936.

## International Rolling Pin & Brick Throwing Contest

When Stroud people emigrated, they named towns in Ontario, Canada; Oklahoma, U.S.A.; and New South Wales, Australia after their original home. In 1960, a Brick Throwing Contest was set up between Stroud, England and Stroud, U.S.A., when it was discovered that both towns had brickworks in common. The other Strouds in Canada and Australia joined in and a rolling pin contest was introduced for the ladies. Once a year on a July day, contestants from Stroud used to compete against each other across the globe. Stroud, UK revived the tradition in 2019 after a break. Stroud, U.S.A and Stroud, Australia still take part. The current brick throwing record is 142'6", and the rolling pin throwing record is 156'4", held by England and U.S.A. respectively.

"Watch out Stanley, there's a rolling pin coming your way!"

Super effort

# The Mill Walk we created

We liked writer Dame Hilary Mantel's thoughts about history. She said "it is what's left in the sieve once the centuries have flowed through it." These fragments are like jigsaw pieces and we became history detectives, searching for clues so we understood the bigger picture.

We decided to create a walk along the Nailsworth valley to see what was left of the mills along a small section of our area. Looking at a Victorian map of 1840, we could see what was there then, compared to now. We stopped at six mills before reaching Dunkirk Mill Centre. We walked along the old railway line, now a cycle path, starting at Sainsbury's and finishing at Egypt Mill.

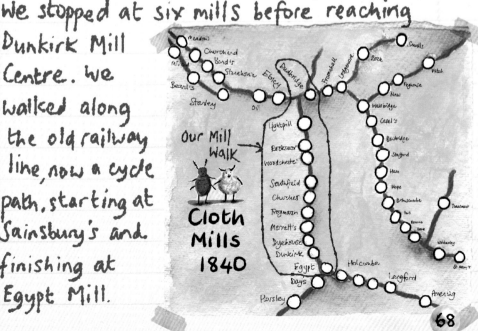

Our Mill Walk

Cloth Mills 1840

Meadow
Iron Mill
Churchend
Beard's
Strehouse
Ebley
Dudbridge
Fromehall
Lodgemore
Rook
Snails
Vatch
Beard's
Staverton
Oil
Peghouse
Neal
Wallbridge
Capel's
Lightpill
Bowbridge
Rooksmoor
Stafford
Woodchester
Ham
Southfield
Hope
Churches
Brimscombe
Frogmarsh
Port
Toadsmoor
Merrett's
Bourne
Dark
Dyehouse
Whiteley
Dunkirk
St Mary's
Egypt
Holcombe
Days
Langford
Avening
Horsley

# Kimmin's or Dudbridge Flour Mills

**History:** Originally Dudbridge Flour Mills built in 1849. By 1873 it was owned by Samuel Marling. It had its own railway siding and is thought to be one of the last and most advanced water - powered flour mills built in Britain.

**Look for** : Two 17th century doorways in the car park. One dated 1646, has the clothier's mark of Daniel Fowler.

# Lightpill Mill

## History:

Used as a cloth mill from the mid 17th century until around 1908. Parts of the mill was used for other purposes: Pin-making from 1834; dyeing from 1855 and printing. In 1911, the mill became one of the earliest British centres of the plastics industry known as Erinoids. It used a German process to create Casein, plastic from protein in cows milk and produced buttons etc.

# Rooksmoor Mill

"It's difficult to imagine Rooksmoor Mill looking like this now!"

History: Earliest record of a cloth mill is in 1729, owned by Thomas Small of Nailsworth, but it's thought there may have been an earlier mill on site. It remained a cloth mill until 1863, when it was occupied by John Grist, a flock and shoddy manufacturer. Fire destroyed many of the buildings in 1935. It was Stroud Flock Company until 1963.

# Woodchester Mill

"This mill had two fires but it's still got its chimney!"

Place on straight grain of fabric

Cutt...
Line...
Ligne...
Schnitt...

History: It's believed this might have been an early fulling mill. A gig mill was recorded here by the 16th century. It was also a grain mill. King George III visited with his wife and three daughters in 1788. By 1901 it was a saw mill but from 1915 until 2003, it was home to Bentley Pianos Ltd, a world-famous piano manufacturer. fires took place in 1804 and 1989.

# Frogmarsh Mill

History: The precise date of the first mill on site is not known. In 1658, it was recorded as being owned and run by Clutterbuck Dean, a Minchinhampton clothier and had two fulling stocks, a gig mill and a dye house. By 1839 no looms were yet recorded implying the mill still relied on cottage weavers. Cloth was made here until 1853. It was then used for pin making.

roundhouse on site once used to dry cloth and store teazles.

# Merrett's Mill

"This rope swing is so much fun!"

"Do be careful Capel!"

History: Merrett's was used as a cloth mill but later turned over to the production of flock, shoddy and mill puff by the Grist family. They had been involved in flock making since 1870, when Mrs. Elizabeth Grist Sons & Co. occupied Capel's Mill. Here they produced mattress wool, mill-puff and manufactured mattresses. The Grists won awards so it was definitely not shoddy work!

# Dunkirk Mill

**History:** Grade II star-listed, this Mill is an impressive monument to Stroud's woollen industry. Earliest reference to a mill here is 1741, described as the New Mills. A five-storey building replaced it. Later owner John Cooper had a gig mill, four fulling stocks as well as picking, shearing and press shops; dye and scouring houses too. Cooper went bankrupt and the Playne family took charge and made cloth until late 1880s. From 1891 walking sticks were made here.

N.B.
Dunkirk has a great heritage centre which we visited. It was amazing!

# Egypt Mill

"They say the guy in charge was so tough, they called him PHARAOH!"

Invite a short sketch about living near a mill in Victorian times. What characters would you have?

**History:** During the 14th century, a small corn mill was established where Egypt Mill is now. Earliest records go back to 1656 when George Hudson, a haberdasher bought it. When he sold it to clothier Richard Webb in 1675, it had two fulling mills, a gig mill and a dye-house. Webb was known as 'Pharaoh', which could explain the name Egypt. Another suggestion is that early Egyptian travellers settled on the river banks. The mill's history includes cloth, logwood and corn milling.

76

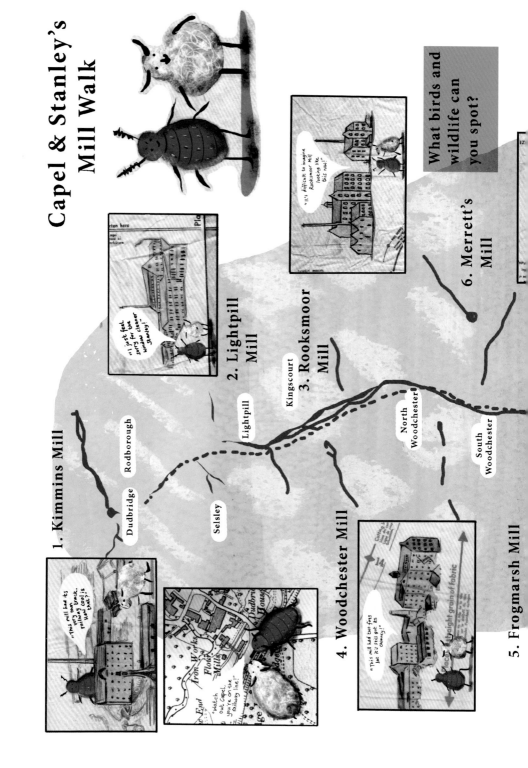

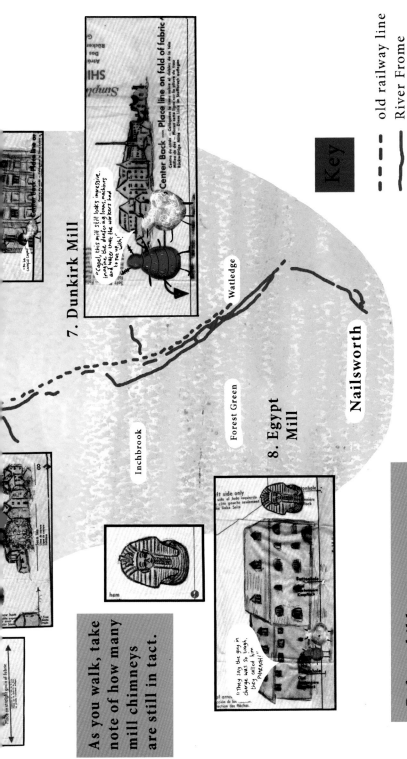

7. Dunkirk Mill

"Capel, this mill still looks impressive, imagine the deafening loom, machines and water that the workers had to put up with."

Watledge

Inchbrook

Forest Green

8. Egypt Mill

Nailsworth

"They say the guy in charge was so tough, they called him 'Pharaoh!'"

As you walk, take note of how many mill chimneys are still in tact.

Before children went to school many helped in the cloth process at home or in the mills.

Key

old railway line

River Frome

Walk distance in miles (5.65 km)

0  1  2  3  3.5

# Art projects based on the mills

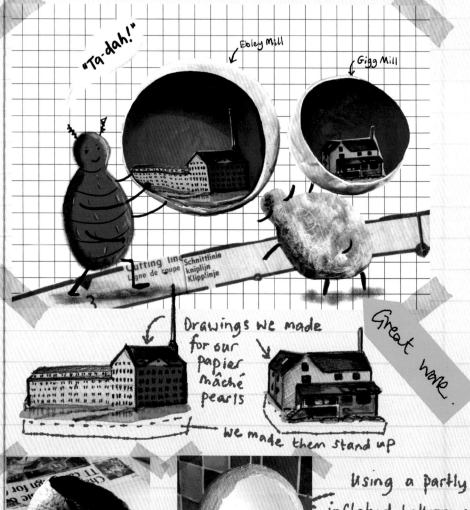

"Ta-dah!"

Ebley Mill

Gigg Mill

Cutting line
Ligne de coupe
Schnittlinie
kniplijn
Klipplinje

Drawings we made for our papier mâché pearls

Great work.

we made them stand up

we popped balloon once dry

Using a partly inflated balloon as a base, we made our papier mâché pearls.

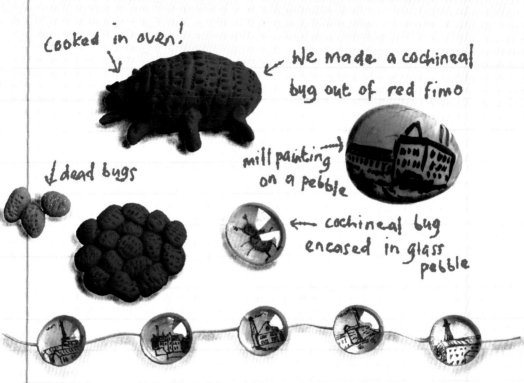

Cooked in oven! ↓

We made a cochineal bug out of red fimo ←

↓ dead bugs

mill painting on a pebble →

← cochineal bug encased in glass pebble

We had great fun making. but we loved our string of pearls the best. We glued drawings of mills to the bottom of glass pebbles so they magnified in size. We were also proud of our funky sheep, made from sticks and wool.

# Wool and mill related sayings

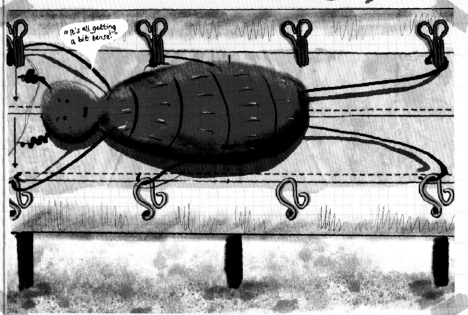

**Pull the wool over one's eyes** - means to deceive, fool, or misdirect someone especially to gain an advantage. Likely refers to a once-common practice when men wore large powdered wigs that resembled lambs' wool.

**Cut one's coat according to one's cloth** - spend only as much money as you can afford. A tailor can only make a coat as big as the cloth he has.

**To go through the mill** - to go through an unpleasant experience in order to gain a skill or degree of knowledge. Cloth-making was arduous but produced a great result.

**To be on tenterhooks** - very nervous, tense or excited about something that is about to happen. Originates from cloth being fastened onto tenters/frames with a sharp hooked nail (a tenterhook).

**Shoddy work** - not up to standard, not very good. Comes from shoddy, made from inferior wool.

**Spinning a yarn** - to tell a story, especially a long made-up imaginative one. Might be of nautical origin from sailors' practice of reminiscing and story-telling while twisting yarn.

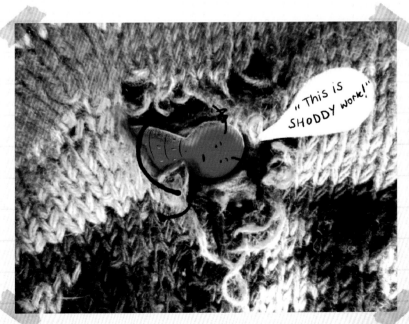

# GLOSSARY

**Apprentice** - person who is learning a trade.

**Bankrupt** - a person or company declared as unable to meet their financial obligations by a court of law.

**Carding** -process of disentangling wool fibres using a metal-toothed or teasel-filled instrument before spinning.

**Combing** - long-fibred wool is combed with metal combs before spinning to help fibres line-up in the direction of the yarn. It makes yarn stronger.

**Clothier** - a person involved in the making and marketing of cloth.

**Emigrate** - to leave one country in order to settle to another one.

**Export** - to send goods or sell goods or raw materials to other countries.

**Fulling** - Process of cleansing, shrinking and thickening cloth with heat, pressure and moisture.

**Imports** - raw materials or goods brought from another country.

**Manufacture** - to make goods.

**Nap** - cloth surface where fibres have been fluffed up from the base of the cloth to give a softer finish covering woven structure of the cloth.

**Revolution** – a significant and relatively sudden change.

**Revolt** – rebellion, or violent action against authority.

**Shuttle** – a bobbin with two pointed ends used for carrying weft threads on a woollen loom, taking it between the warp threads.

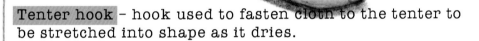

**Tenter hook** – hook used to fasten cloth to the tenter to be stretched into shape as it dries.

**Tenter rack** – piece of equipment to stretch cloth into shape as it dries.

**Textiles industry** – the large industry involved in making cloth and other materials woven from fibres.

**Warp** – yarn that is fixed to the loom in direction of the fabric length. The weft yarn is passed between the warps during weaving which have to be strong enough to withstand tension on the loom.

**Weaving** – interlacing material threads as a method of making fabric such as wool or cotton.

**Weft** – yarn that is woven across the warps on the loom during weaving.

**Strike** – refusal to work by a group of employees as a form of protest.

# TIMELINE

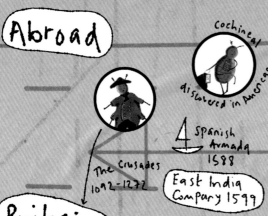

Cochineal discovered in Americas

Seven Years war
1756-63

War of Independence 17

Boston T Party 177

BOW
EUD PA
CORBATA E LAZ
KRAWATTENBAND

CIT 2
COUREZ
CORTE 2
2 ZUSCH

The Crusades
1092-1272

Spanish Armada
1588

East India Company 1599

## Britain

Black Death
1348-1350

English Civil War
1642-51

1st canal in UK
1741

Industrial

Factory Act
1733

IE
DOBLEZ
PLURE
EL DOBLE

## Stroud

First Fulling Mills

First scarlet used
1712

Domesday Survey
1068

Middle Ages, Tudors, Stuarts etc

George I
1714

George II
1727

George III
1760

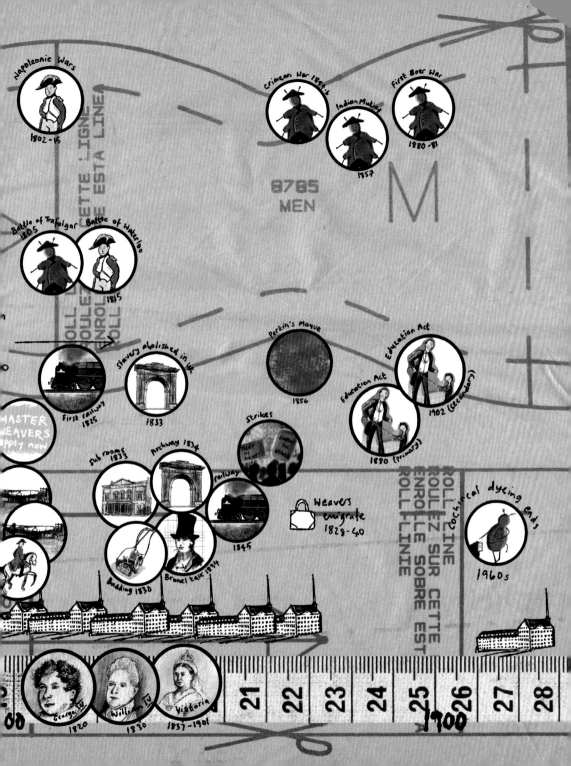

Napoleonic Wars
1802–15

Crimean War 1854–6

Indian Mutiny
1857

First Boer War
1880–81

8785
MEN

M

Battle of Trafalgar
1805

Battle of Waterloo
1815

ROLL
ROULEZ CETTE LIGNE
ENROLE ESTA LINEA
ROLL

ROLL
ROULEZ
ENROL
ROLL

Perkin's Mauve
1856

Education Act

Education Act
1902 (secondary)

First railway
1825

Slavery abolished in UK
1833

Strikes
TREAT US FAIRER   SUPPORT THE WEAVERS

1880 (primary)

MASTER
WEAVERS
apply now

Sub rooms
1833

Archway 1834

railway

Weavers
emigrate
1828–40

ROLL LINE
ROULEZ SUR CETTE
ENROLE SOBRE EST
ROLL LINIE

Cochineal dyeing ends

1960s

Budding 1830

Brunel talk 1834

1845

George IV
1820

William IV
1830

Victoria
1837–1901

21  22  23  24  25  26  27  28

1900

# Looking back

Sometimes we forget that life was so different for people (bugs and sheep). Now we have a better understanding, every time we see a mill chimney, a mill pond, waterwheel or mill, we can imagine what it was like and the activity that took place inside. When residents and visitors

"It was worth it"

PLEASE LOOK AFTER THIS BUG Thank you

read about Stroud's important woollen and industrial heritage, perhaps they will think about the tiny South American bug which gave the town its rich scarlet dye; the weavers; the scribblers; the carders; the teasle-gig workers; the shearers and don't forget the poor chap who had to collect all the wee from the cottages. It was a very important ingredient in the early days. We must also remember the unfortunate souls who would have had to spend hours and hours walking on cloth in that very substance! They would have easily clocked up 10,000 steps a day. Needless to say we are both proud of the parts we played in Stroud's history.

# And finally... what became of us?

In the 1800s...

Stanley's cousins, the merinos of Australia arrived. It was not good news for him. Their wool was brighter and better for felting so he was replaced and given his notice. Poor Stanley. He spent the rest of his days munching grass, dozing and counting sheep.

In the 1960s...

Capel, on the other hand, had a role to play in Stroud for much longer. Even though synthetic dyes were all the rage from the Victorian era, cochineal could not be produced easily using this method, so Capel's family provided scarlet dye until the 1960s. She then became a hippy, got married to a gorgeous bug, had a few mini bugs and travelled the world.

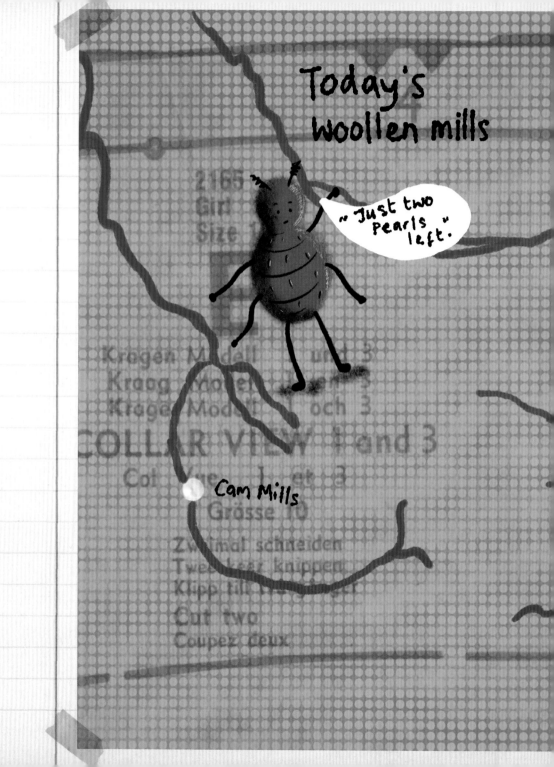

# Thank you

It's a thank you from her (Capel) and a thank you from him (Stanley).

You can now understand why we are proud of Stroud.

Don't forget us!

# A small note about our artistic director:

Tracy Spiers is an illustrator and writer with a passion for telling stories about history in a playful, engaging and colourful way. Married to Rog, with five daughters, she can often be spotted running along the Cotswold canal paths, drawing and drinking cappuccinos. Small with a big imagination, she often dyes her hair bright colours, including red, however emphasises Capel and her chums are not harmed during the process.

To find out more visit: www.tracyspiers.com

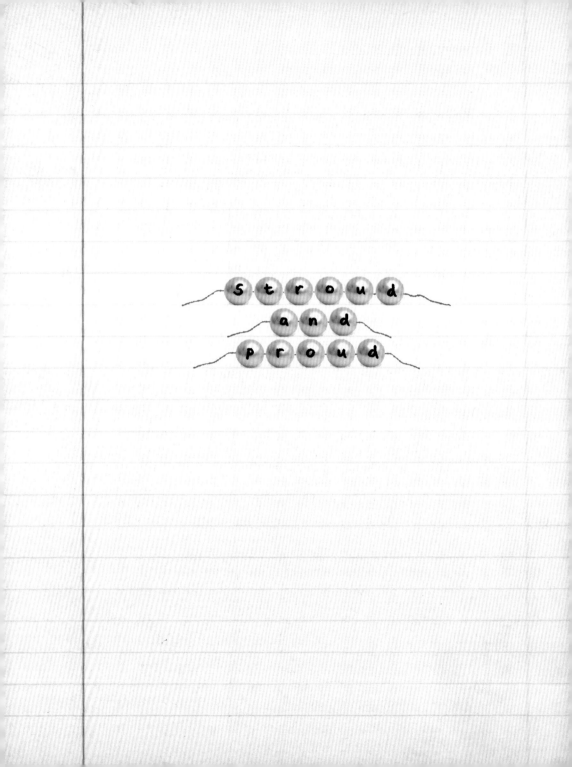